Money Management

by Connor Stratton

FOCUS READERS
PIONEER

www.focusreaders.com

Focus Readers is distributed by North Star Editions:
sales@northstareditions.com | 888-417-0195

Produced for Focus Readers by Red Line Editorial.

Photographs ©: Shutterstock Images, cover, 1, 4, 6, 8, 10 (top), 10 (bottom), 12, 14 (top), 14 (bottom), 17, 18, 21

Library of Congress Cataloging-in-Publication Data
Names: Stratton, Connor, author.
Title: Money management / Connor Stratton.
Description: Lake Elmo, MN : Focus Readers, [2023] | Series: Exploring
  money | Includes index. | Audience: Grades 2-3
Identifiers: LCCN 2022001363 (print) | LCCN 2022001364 (ebook) | ISBN
  9781637392386 (hardcover) | ISBN 9781637392904 (paperback) | ISBN
  9781637393932 (pdf) | ISBN 9781637393420 (ebook)
Subjects: LCSH: Money--Juvenile literature. | Budgets, Personal--Juvenile
  literature. | Finance, Personal--Juvenile literature.
Classification: LCC HG221.5 .S87 2023 (print) | LCC HG221.5 (ebook) | DDC
  332.4--dc23/eng/20220112
LC record available at https://lccn.loc.gov/2022001363
LC ebook record available at https://lccn.loc.gov/2022001364

Printed in the United States of America
Mankato, MN
082022

About the Author

Connor Stratton writes and edits nonfiction children's books. Growing up, he helped his dad collect the 50 State Quarters.

Table of Contents

Chapter 1

Money Matters

Money is important for many people. They **spend** money on things they need. Food, clothing, and housing all cost money.

People also spend money on things they want. Toys and trips cost money.

People earn money by working. Then they can spend their money. They can **save** some of it, too.

Chapter 2

Managing Money

People don't want to run out of money. So, they keep track of it. That way, they have enough money for all their needs.

Suppose a girl needs $10 for a meal. She has $12. But she buys a toy for $4. That leaves her with only $8. Now she doesn't have enough for the meal. Next time, the girl can **manage** her money better.

Did You Know? People often save large amounts of money in **banks**.

Chapter 3

About Budgets

Budgets can help people manage money. A budget tracks two things. First, it shows **sources** of money. Jobs are common sources.

COMPANY INC.
123 Street Name
City Name, CA 90000

Cheque No: 123456
Client No: 12345

Date: January 10, 2013

Pay against this cheque   Amount: USD 10247.40
To   Current Name   Company Name
      Street Name, City   Or Order

The Sum of   TEN THOUTHANDS TWO HUNDRED AND FOURTY SEVEN 40/100 U.S. DOLLARS

Payable at   Bank Name   For: Bank Branch Name
              Street Name
              City Name, CA 90000

                                            Authorised Signature

Next, a budget shows spending. It lists the cost of each item. A budget puts the sources next to the spending. That way, people can keep track. They can make better choices about money. They might decide to spend less on treats. Or they might put more in savings.

App Savers

Many people want to save money. But life can get very busy. People don't always remember to set money aside. Banking **apps** can help. These apps can save money **automatically**. People choose how much they want to save. Then the app sets the money aside in a bank. That way, people don't need to remember.

Chapter 4

Using a Budget

Budgets help people meet their needs. Suppose a girl earns $2 for every chore. She needs money for sandals. She wants a new book, too. She also wants to build her savings.

So, the girl makes a budget. She lists the chores as her sources of money. Then she lists the book and sandals as spending. The girl subtracts the spending costs from what she earned doing chores. She puts the remaining money into savings.

Sources:
Do laundry (twice) $4
Sweep (twice) $4
Dust shelves (twice) $4
Vacuum $2
Rake $2
Total: $16

Spending:
Book $4
Sandals $10
Total: $14

$16-$14=$2 into savings

FOCUS ON
Money Management

Write your answers on a separate piece of paper.

1. Write a sentence that explains the main idea of Chapter 2.

2. Would using a budget help you manage your money? Why or why not?

3. A job is an example of what?

    A. spending money

    B. source of money

    C. saving money

4. Suppose you make $10 a month. Your spending adds up to $8 a month. How much money do you have left each month for your savings?

    A. $2

    B. $10

    C. $18

Answer key on page 24.

Glossary

apps
Computer programs that complete tasks.

automatically
Done on its own, without any outside control.

banks
Places that keep people's money safe.

budgets
Tools that help people keep track of how much they save and spend.

manage
To handle or control something.

save
To set money aside so it can be used later.

sources
Places where things come from.

spend
To use money to pay for something.

To Learn More

BOOKS

Gaertner, Meg. *Spending and Saving Money.* Minneapolis: Abdo Publishing, 2018.

Huddleston, Emma. *Managing Money.* Lake Elmo, MN: Focus Readers, 2021.

NOTE TO EDUCATORS

Visit **www.focusreaders.com** to find lesson plans, activities, links, and other resources related to this title.

Index

Answer Key: 1. Answers will vary; **2.** Answers will vary; **3.** B; **4.** A